Night Picnic

Also by Charles Simic

Night Picnic

Poems

Charles Simic

Harcourt, Inc.

NEW YORK   SAN DIEGO   LONDON

www.harcourt.com

Library of Congress Cataloging-in-Publication Data
Simic, Charles, 1938–
Night picnic: poems/Charles Simic.—1st ed.
p.   cm.
ISBN 0-15-100630-X
I. Title.
PS3569.I4725 N54 2001
811'.54—dc21   2001024100

Text set in New Baskerville

First edition
K J I H G F E D C B A

Printed in the United States of America

Contents

Part I

Do you want to hear about the ants in my pants
For a certain Ms. Hopeless?

Or do you prefer me singing Amazing Grace?

Past-Lives Therapy

They explained to me the bloody bandages
On the floor in the maternity ward in Rochester, N.Y.
Cured the backache I acquired bowing to my old master,
Made me stop putting thumbtacks round my bed.

They showed me an officer on horseback,
Waving a saber next to a burning farmhouse
And a barefoot woman in a nightgown,
Throwing stones after him and calling him Lucifer.

I was a straw-headed boy in patched overalls.
Come dark a chicken would roost in my hair.
Some even laid eggs as I played my ukulele
And my mother and father crossed themselves.

Next, I saw myself inside an abandoned gas station
Constructing a spaceship out of a coffin,
Red traffic cone, cement mixer and ear warmers,
When a church lady fainted seeing me in my underwear.

Some days, however, they opened door after door,
Always to a different room, and could not find me.
There'd be only a small squeak now and then,
As if a miner's canary got caught in a mousetrap.

Street of Jewelers

What each one of these hundreds
Of windows did with the gold
That was melting in them this morning,
I cannot begin to imagine.

I act like a prospective burglar
Noting the ones that are open,
Their curtains drawn to the side
By someone stark naked,
I may have just missed.

Here, where no one walks now,
And when he does, he goes softly,
So as not to tip the scales
In the act of weighing
Specks of dust in the dying sunlight.

Three Doors

This one kept its dignity
Despite being kicked
And smudged with fingerprints.

Someone wanted to get in
Real bad.
Now the whole neighborhood can see
What went on late last night
And the night before.

Two clenched fists
Raised high
Pounding, pounding,
And asking God
To please bear witness.

☾

This door's hinges,
I suspect,
Give off a nasty screech
From seeing
Too many feet caught in it.

Just a minute ago,
Some fellow
With that it-pays-to-be-cagey look
Snuck out.

Screams of a child,
Yelps of a kicked dog
And wild laughter
Followed after him.

☽

I heard the neighbor's screen door
Creak open at daybreak
To let the cat in
With what sounded like a stage whisper
Into her still-dark kitchen.

I could feel the black cat rub herself
Against her bare legs
And then take her first lick
With her rough, red tongue
Of the cold milk glowing in the saucer.

The Avenue of Earthly Delights

Hustlers of gold chains,
Coming our way in the midnight crowd,
Waving them up high
Like angry rattlesnakes.
A French-kissing couple
Falling on the hood of a braking taxi,
Still holding on to their drinks.

Large and small African masks
On a makeshift table
With empty eye sockets,
Mouths frozen in a scream
A tangle of tanned arms, breasts
Bathed in sweat slipping out
Of a strapless dress,

Short skirt like shreds of tinfoil
Fluttering in an electric fan
As she executes a dance step,
Fingers popping, tongue sticking out
As if this sultry night
Was a delicious, creamy dessert,
And we were all shortly due
To hop into one big haystack,

Dallying into the wee hours
And the soft light of day—
Which dares not come—
With its funny side streets
And the homeless, fallen off their crosses,
Sprawled in dark doorways.

Couple at Coney Island

It was early one Sunday morning,
So we put on our best rags
And went for a stroll along the boardwalk
Till we came to a kind of palace
With turrets and pennants flying.
It made me think of a wedding cake
In the window of a fancy bakery shop.

I was warm, so I took my jacket off
And put my arm round your waist
And drew you closer to me
While you leaned your head on my shoulder,
Anyone could see we'd made love
The night before and were still giddy on our feet.
We looked naked in our clothes

Staring at the red and white pennants
Whipped by the sea wind.
The rides and shooting galleries
With their ducks marching in line
Still boarded up and padlocked.
No one around yet to take our first dime.

Angel Tongue

Theresa, do you recall that dive
Smoke-filled like a house on fire
Where nightly we huddled
In one of the rear booths
Reading to each other from a book
On the mystic way of life?

You worked in a bridal shop
With iron bars on its windows.
The two brides on display
Had tense little smiles for me
Every time I stopped by
While you peeked between them
All prim and rosy-cheeked.

We played an elaborate game
Of hide-and-seek with words
While pretending to find clues
Of divine presence in streets
Emptied at day's end, dark
But for the sight of your lips
Quivering from the cold

As you told me of *a light*
So fine, so rare, it lights
The very light we see by.
In the meantime, your eyes were
Open so wide, I hurried
To close them with kisses,
While you ranted about mystic death
With the tongue of an angel.

Unmade Beds

They like shady rooms,
Peeling wallpaper,
Cracks on the ceiling,
Flies on the pillow.

If you are tempted to lie down,
Don't be surprised,
You won't mind the dirty sheets,
The rasp of rusty springs
As you make yourself comfy.
The room is a darkened movie theater
Where a grainy,
Black-and-white film is being shown.

A blur of disrobed bodies
In the moment of sweet indolence
That follows lovemaking,
When the meanest of hearts
Comes to believe
Happiness can last forever.

Firecracker Time

I was drumming on my bald head with a pencil,
Making a list of my sins. Well, not exactly.
I was in bed smoking a cigar and studying
The news photo of a Jesus lookalike
Who won a pie-eating contest in Texas.

Is there some unsuspected dignity to this foolishness?
I inquired of the newly painted ceiling.
Is someone about to slip a note under my door
Summoning me urgently to a meeting
With the Pope in a room down the hall?

Hell, I may only be the boatman Charon,
Ruined by a new bridge over the river Styx!
It was almost the year 2000, so I dialed room service.
Send me Miss Atlantic City 1964.
If she's unavailable, send me a talking dog!

Nobody answered. There was a politician on TV
It would be a real pleasure to spit at in person.
Over the rooftops eeriness loomed large,
Small, baleful gusts whipped the trash in the street
And vacancy signs hung everywhere.

Sunday Papers

The butchery of the innocent
Never stops. That's about all
We can ever be sure of, love,
Even more sure than the roast
You are bringing out of the oven.

It's Sunday. The congregation
Files slowly out of the church
Across the street. A good many
Carry Bibles in their hands.
It's the vague desire for truth
And the mighty fear of it
That makes them turn up
Despite the glorious spring weather.

In the hallway, the old mutt
Just now had the honesty
To growl at his own image in the mirror,
Before lumbering off to the kitchen
Where the lamb roast sat
In your outstretched hands
Smelling of garlic and rosemary.

Cherry Blossom Time

Gray sewage bubbling up out of street sewers
After the spring rain with the clear view
Of hawkers of quack remedies and their customers
Swarming on the Capitol steps.

At the National Gallery the saints' tormented faces
Suddenly made sense.
Several turned their eyes on me
As I stepped over the shiny parquetry.

And who and what was I, if you please?
A minor provincial grumbler on a holiday,
With hands clasped behind his back
Nodding to everyone he meets

As if this was a 1950s Fall of the Roman Empire movie
    set,
And we the bewildered,
Absurdly costumed, milling extras
Among the pink cherry blossoms.

People Eating Lunch

And thinking with each mouthful,
Or so it appears, seated as they are
At the coffee shop counter, biting
Into thick sandwiches, chewing
And deliberating carefully before taking
Another small sip of their sodas.

The gray-haired counterman
Taking an order has stopped to ponder
With a pencil paused over his pad,
The fellow in a blue baseball cap
And the woman wearing dark glasses
Are both thoroughly baffled
As they stir and stir their coffees.

If they should look up, they may see
Socrates himself bending over the grill
In a stained white apron and a hat
Made out of yesterday's newspaper,
Tossing an omelet philosophically,
In a small frying pan blackened with fire.

Sweet Tooth

Take her to that pastry shop on Lexington.
Let her sample cream puffs at the counter,
The peach tarts on the street.
If topping or filling spurts down her chin,
Or even better, down her cleavage,

Lick it off before it dribbles down her dress.
With people going by, some pretending
Not to see you, while others stall,
Blinking as if the sun was in their eyes
Or they've left their glasses at home.

The uniformed schoolgirls, holding hands
In pairs, on their way to the park,
Are turning their heads, too, and so are
The red-faced men humping sides of beef
Out a freezer truck into a fancy butcher shop

While she continues to choke on an éclair,
Stopping momentarily with a mouthful
To wince at a brand-new stain on her skirt,
Which you've no time to attend to,
Giving all your devotion to the one higher up.

The One to Worry About

I failed miserably at imagining nothing.
Something always came to keep me company:
A small nameless bug crossing the table,
The memory of my mother, the ringing in my ear.
I was distracted and perplexed.
A hole is invariably a hole in something.

About seven this morning, a lone beggar
Waited for me with his small, sickly dog
Whose eyes grew bigger on seeing me.
There goes, the eyes said, that nice man
To whom (appearances to the contrary)
Nothing in this whole wide world is sacred.

I was still a trifle upset entering the bakery
When an unknown woman stepped out
Of the back to wait on me dressed for a night
On the town in a low-cut, tight-fitting black dress.
Her face was solemn, her eyes averted,
While she placed a muffin in my hand,
As if all along she knew what I was thinking.

The Golden Age of Opera

One evening I turned to address the wall
As if it were both my judge
And jury, and I both the accused
And his lawyer, asking questions,
Demanding answers wearing only my shorts

Because of the heat, getting so irate,
I fell silent for long periods
Glaring into space, and then again
At the wall, with that I-couldn't-care-less
Look it has—the indignity of it all!

With the city boiling in its bloody stew,
Ambulances, fire engines, cops on wheels.
Then, in the thick of it, the sound of opera
On a scratchy record in the next apartment,
A high soprano chirping about love.

Every last one of them raving mad, surely,
The tenor's pleading voice broken by sobs,
The cars' headlights on the avenue making
My shadow on the wall leap back and forth
With hands pressed hard against its ears.

The Improbable

There may be words left
On the blackboard
In that gray schoolhouse
Shut for the winter break.

Someone was called upon
To wipe them off
And then the bell rang,
The eraser stayed where it was
Next to the chalk.

None of them knew
You'd be passing by this morning
With your eyes raised
As if recollecting
With a thrill of apprehension

About the improbable
That alone makes us possible
As it makes you possible
In this fleeting moment
Before the lights change.

My Father Attributed Immortality to Waiters

for DEREK WALCOTT

For surely, there's no difficulty in understanding
The unreality of an occasional customer
Such as ourselves seated at one of the many tables
As pale as the cloth that covers them.

Time in its augmentations and diminutions,
Does not concern these two in the least.
They stand side by side facing the street,
Wearing identical white jackets and fixed smiles,

Ready to incline their heads in welcome
Should one of us come through the door
After reading the high-priced menu on this street
Of many hunched figures and raised collars.

Window Decorator

I see you put Christmas lights
And a tree in the window
Of a funeral home. Very nice,
I say. There are even teased
Wads of white cotton
To make us think of snow,
From the same stash, I suppose,
You plug ears and noses with.

Lord knows what else
You've got waiting for us beyond
The heavy, ornate door.
Santa's beard for grandma
Laid out in her coffin?
A new sled for some little girl
And even a lone snowflake
Freshly fallen on her sleeping cheek?

Part II

The Altar

The plastic statue of the Virgin
On top of a bedroom dresser
With a blackened mirror
From a bad-dream grooming salon.

Two pebbles from the grave of a rock star,
A small, grinning windup monkey,
A bronze Egyptian coin
And a red movie-ticket stub.

A splotch of sunlight on the framed
Communion photograph of a boy
With the eyes of someone
Who will drown in a lake real soon.

An altar dignifying the god of chance.
What is beautiful, it cautions,
Is found accidentally and not sought after.
What is beautiful is easily lost.

Bible Lesson

There's another, better world
Of divine love and benevolence,
A mere breath away
From this grubby vacant lot
With its exposed sewer pipe,
Rats hatching plots in broad daylight,
Young boys in leather jackets
Showing each other their knives.

"A necessary evil, my dear child,"
The old woman told me with a sigh,
Taking another sip of her sherry.
For birds warbling back and forth
In their gold cage in the parlor,
She had a teary-eyed reverence.
"Angelic", she called them,
May she roast in a trash fire
The homeless warm their hands over,

While beyond the flimsiest partition
The blessed ones stroll in a garden,
Their voices tuned to a whisper
As they dab their eyes
With the hems of their white robes
And opine in their tactful way
On the news of long freight trains
Hauling men and women
Deeper into the century's darkness.

For the Very Soul of Me

At the close of a sweltering night,
I found him at the entrance
Of a tower made of dark blue glass,
Crumpled on his side, naked,
Shielding his crotch with both hands,
His rags rolled up into a pillow.

The missing one, missed by no one,
Bruised and crusted with dirt,
As all the truly destitute are
Who make their bed on the bare pavement.
His mouth open as in death,
Or in memory of some debauchery.

The city at this hour tiptoe-quiet,
A lone yellow cab idling at the light,
The sleep-woozy driver taking a breath
Of the passing breeze,
Cool and smelling of the sea.

Insomnia and heat drove me out early,
Made me turn down one block
And not another, as if running
With a hot cinder in my eye,
And see him lying there unclothed,
One leg quivering now and then.

I thought, What if the cops find him?
So I looked up and down the avenue,
All the way to where the pyre
Of the sunrise had turned the sky red,
For something to cover him with.

Stand-In

Before they strapped him in a jacket
And stuffed his mouth with a rag,
He slipped into the empty church,
Climbed the high, dim-lit cross,
And clasped the suffering Jesus.

All naked himself, clinging on tight,
The fucker. Thus, the pious found him,
And ran out for help, leaving him
With one candle already sputtering
Beneath his swollen, homeless feet.

The Devil Minds His Own Children

In the back of a toy store
He took his time
Trying last year's Halloween masks.
The expression of alarm
On the saleslady's face
Concerned the ceiling
Where a red balloon had popped.

The pale Frankenstein,
His black stitches
About to rupture in his head—.
Aha, someone said,
While he brushed past her
And out into the pouring rain.

Demonology

The devil's got his finger in every pie,
Ask around, if you don't believe me.
Better yet, turn on the TV for confirmation:
The flames and smoke over the schoolhouse
Had his signature in the evening sky.

I want a bite of your immortal soul,
See if it cracks like burnt toast, she whispered
Stubbing a butt on her plate.
And I want to see your tail, I replied,
While watching the ambulance door open

Through the crook of her bare arm,
With the sound off and the gray rain
Beginning to tap on the windowpane.
Afterwards, I thought I could see
A run of teeny black devils in my urine.

Sleepwalkers

You meet them in broad daylight
Fully dressed moving with the crowd.
Their eyes may be wide open,
But they do not see anyone,
Nor do they catch sight of themselves
In dusty store windows
Drifting in the company of white clouds.

One of them crossing the avenue
Carried on his back a long bedroll
With something heavy in it
Protruding, laterally, cross-like.
The idlers, gathered to watch a fire-eater,
The puffed-up pigeons
Strutting between their feet,
Turned to follow him with their eyes.

I had no choice but to trail along,
Terrified at his sudden lurches,
How he almost dropped on one knee
Before the girl in a short red skirt
And white leather boots
Who awoke with a start and stared
At his face streaked with grime
As if he were Jesus Christ himself.

And Then I Think

I'm just a storefront dentist
Extracting a blackened tooth at midnight.

I chewed on many bitter truths, Doc,
My patient says after he spits the blood out

Still slumped over, gray-haired
And smelling of carrion just like me.

Of course, I may be the only one here,
And this is a mirror trick I'm performing.

Even the few small crumpled bills
He leaves on the way out, I don't believe in.

I may pluck them with a pair of wet pincers
And count them, and then I may not.

Leaving an Unknown City

That mutt with ribs showing
We saw standing near a garbage truck
With a most hopeful look,
His tail on the verge of happiness
As the train picked up speed
The outcome left open

With the night falling rapidly
Making the dusty windows reflect
Our five traveling companions
Sitting with hat-shrouded eyes,
The absentminded smiles
Already firmly set on each face.

Views From a Train

Then there's aesthetic paradox
Which notes that someone else's tragedy
Often strikes the casual viewer
With the feeling of happiness.

There was the sight of squatters' shacks,
Naked children and lean dogs running
On what looked like a town dump,
The smallest one hopping after them on crutches.

All of a sudden we were in a tunnel.
The wheels ground our thoughts,
Back and forth as if they were gravel.
Before long we found ourselves on a beach,
The water blue, the sky cloudless.

Seaside villas, palm trees, white sand;
A woman in a red bikini waved to us
As if she knew each one of us
Individually and was sorry to see us
Heading so quickly into another tunnel.

Along With the Name Came His Shadow

He was Icarus's dog, letting the whole world know
From the top of a cliff
What he thought of his master's stunt.
People threw pebbles, but he stayed put
Long after there was nothing more to see.
A steamy, late-summer listlessness
Spread over the sea and the sky.
Not even one gull to commemorate the event.

He called it quits. Barking one's heart out
Is one sure way to ease one's mind.
He loped down the narrow, winding path
Sniffing around the scraggly bushes,
Stopping only to pee blissfully.
Down on the beach, with his tail wagging
He grew smaller and smaller
Until there was nothing but white sand.

Book Lice

Dust-covered Gideon Bibles
In musty drawers of slummy motels,
Is what they love to dine on.
O eternities, moments divine!
Munching on pages edged in gold
While the thin-legged suicide
Draws her steaming bath,
Her face already blurring in the mirror,
And the gray-haired car thief
Presses his eyes shut on a windowpane
Pockmarked with the evening rain.

Madge Put On Your Teakettle

We are being bamboozled,
That's pretty obvious.
The bumblebees making their rounds,
The lone sparrow
Hopping back and forth nonchalantly
In front of the tiger cat
Sprawled on the new grass.

There's nothing to worry about,
The leaves are whispering.
Your own shadow sits in silent study
Of an empty spiderweb.
Two ants hauling a dead cricket
To a cricket cemetery
Have stopped to scratch their heads.

The Loons

By the force of their imaginings
They'd change from men to women,
And women again to men,
Not to forget dogs, asses, chickens.

In that little burg where they hoodwink
One another, dupe, beguile
The visitor, the road seemed moonstruck
In broad daylight.

The country store with a porch sold loons
Made out of blocks of wood
The same dead-set, loony look
Replicated in hundreds of eyes.

The chuckling boy who pumped gas
Held a tomcat under his other arm.
Did the two know what they were?
Loons, I shouted at them, as I drove off.

The Secret of the Yellow Room

Sloth's best. Lolling on a sofa
In a Chinese dressing gown
With the windows open to the heat,
The breeze rousing the leaves.
The flies dozing on the ceiling.

The silky hush of a summer afternoon,
Like floating with eyes closed
On one's back in a pond
Clogged with water lilies
And inhaling their scent as they nuzzle close.

The light and shade dally
On the ceiling, the leaves sigh once—
Afterwards, not even that.
Majestic stupor. Stirring only at midnight
To click on the yellow table lamp.

Dog on a Chain

So, that's how it's going to be,
A gray afternoon smelling of snow.
Step around the bare oak tree
And see how quickly you get
Yourself entangled for good?
Your bad luck was being friendly
With people who love their new couch
More than they love you.

Fred, you poor mutt, the night
Is falling. The children playing
Across the road were cold,
So they ran in. Watch the smoke
Swirl out of their chimney
In the windy sky as long as you're able.
Soon, no one will see you sitting there.
You'll have to bark even if
There's no moon, bark and growl
To keep yourself company.

Burning Edgar Allan Poe

O the late days of autumn,
The wind's blowing
Charred book pages
Out of a neighbor's chimney
Scaring the blackbirds.
They can't tell their own
From the flying soot
In the saffron-colored sky,
And neither can I.

The Cemetery

Dark nights, there were lovers
To stake out among the tombstones.
If the moon slid out of the clouds,
We saw more while ducking out of sight,

A mound of dirt beside a dug grave.
Oh God! the mound cried out.
There were ghosts about
And rats feasting on the white cake
Someone had brought that day,

With flies unzipped we lay close,
Straining to hear the hot, muffled words
That came quicker and quicker,
Back then when we still could
Bite our tongues and draw blood.

Summer in the Country

One shows me how to lie down in a field of clover.
Another how to slip my hand under her Sunday skirt.
Another how to kiss with a mouth full of blackberries.
Another how to catch fireflies in a jar after dark.

Here is a stable with a single black mare
and the proof of God's existence riding in a red
    nightgown.
Devil's child—or whatever she was.
Having the nerve to ask me to go get her a whip.

I Climbed a Tree to Make Sure

A working slaughterhouse prettied up
By the evening sunlight
Is what I think of your meadows and hills,
Mrs. Simic.

What about the woods in the back
Where your cats vanish
And one hears short, bloodcurdling
Shrieks at night—or worse!
One hears nothing
But the wind gusting in the dry leaves—
Like a baby rattle
Shaken by an undertaker?

Every butcher needs an assistant,
The sun skewered in a tree told me.
By now I could smell your chimney smoke,
And before long there you were,
Stirring the heavy pot on the stove,
Turning around to wink at me.

The Truth About Us

The crow struts back and forth
Over the fresh roadkill
While the shade trees bend over him
With a mourner's courtesy.
That's the truth for you!
The rest is imposture,
Bedtime stories, sweet lies
Of sunlight in the eyes,

That made my young neighbor
Take off her shirt in the garden
And stretch her arms to the sky
As if to beguile me further,
While I shuddered and raised
The collar of my overcoat
At the sight of a long white worm
Crawling out of the roses.

Roadside Stand

In the watermelon and corn season,
The earth is a paradise, the morning
Is a ripe plum or a plump tomato
We bite into as if it were the mouth of a lover.

Despite the puzzled face of the young fellow
In scarecrow overalls reading a comic book,
It's all there, the bell peppers, the radishes,
Local blueberries and blackberries
That will stain our lips and tongues
As if we were freezing to death in the snow.

The kid is bored, or pretends to be,
While watching the woman pick up a melon
And press its rough skin against her cheek.
What makes people happy is a mystery,
He concludes as he busies himself
Straightening crumpled bills in a cigar box.

New Red Sneakers

A lifetime of sleepless nights
Cannot alter the course of events.
Still, when has that ever
Stopped any one of us from trying, my friend?
Or so I told the dog trailing after me.

The fields and orchards were in flower.
The road we were walking
Wound laggardly through their lushness
In no rush to reach a destination.
My heart was a sparrow chirping
On a fresh pile of horse shit.

Happiness on all fronts!
Except for the two crows up ahead
Cooling their heels in anticipation
Of one of us being run over by a car.
It made the poor mutt tear after them
In furious pursuit, accompanied by
A righteous bark, that said it all!

Grand Theatrics

I went down on my knees
And begged
Miss Hands-on-Her-Hips
For one little treat
Out of the folds
Of her loose-fitting robe,
Short and belted
Negligently at the waist.

A lick at the cross
Between her titties,
Perhaps?
While she dangled
One red slipper in midair,
Her get-the-hell-out-of-here-
And-go-to-work,
Coming in short gasps.

The Number of Fools

Is infinite, said my love,
Quoting Solomon,
Which made me see stars,
The vastness of the universe.
The one who is not a fool
Like a sugar cube that fell in the sea.
The one who is not a fool
Like a tarantula
On a slice of wedding cake—
So I covered my ears.

Tree of Subtleties

The leaves of that tree in the yard,
If you ask me, are hinting
At dark secrets still to be unveiled,
Even on this brightest of mornings
With the sun's yellow broom
Sweeping the corners for leftover gloom.

No matter. Weighted with obscurities,
Telling of a dark night of the soul,
Making my heart flutter
As if St. John of the Cross himself
Was whispering his verses
To the white chickens pecking the corn.

Jar of Fireflies

In the first dark,
Someone is there
Under the trees.

The hands flare
And the face.
But not long enough
To see who it is.

That is why I listen
For approaching steps
And hear only
The wind worrying
The dark leaves.

We Were Adding and Subtracting

Golden bars of sunlight on the floor
Of the one-room schoolhouse
Made a birdcage
Where the wooden benches once stood.
I may have sat in one of them
Only yesterday,
Watching the dust motes float
Toward a corner that stayed dark.

A large room with no hiding places
Where I strove to make myself invisible,
And then one day finally did.
The school bell at the end of a long rope
Rang in the yard
As if someone had hung himself—
And wouldn't you know it!
Somebody actually went out and did.

With Heart Racing

Give yourself over to the moment
Now that you've found refuge
From the sudden downpour
Under these low-hanging shade trees.

Listen to the loud pinpricks
As if a dreamy, absentminded seamstress
Were stitching together
Time and eternity for you.

In the watery, emerald green light
Of the late afternoon,
The leaves, too, finding it hard
Not to shudder a little
As they give ear to the rain.

Part III

The Grand Casino

Gambling casino of the sky
Lit up with summer stars.

That's the soul's jukebox,
We are told by the night wind.

But when we ask what size coin it takes
We are greeted with stunned silence.

In Solitary

It took courage, eh?
To tap on the wall
After the lights were out
In hopes
You'd be overheard by someone

In this clink
We call the world,
Where the turnkey
Is so discreet
No one has yet seen him.

The firm taps
Spelling out a name,
The years of confinement—
Or something else?

I dozed off thinking,
And when I came to,
I heard my heartbeat
And nothing else.

In the Rathole

Mouth, old rathole
From which the words
Scurry after dark

Back inside my head—
Where else?
I ask you, where else?

☾

I'm whittling a crutch
In your walls
For a brother rat
Whose leg I bit.

☾

My narrow bed's
Asthmatic wheeze,
How well you must know it
In your insomnia,

As I toss and turn,
Mulling over
What beauty, what beast
You bait my trap with.

☾

Light,
Mystic tipster,
You come rarely,
If at all

Down in the hole
To see me kneeling
With a clip-on halo
Waiting for you.

☾

Grand soirees of grotesqueries
Twitching my greasy whiskers
In front of a mirror,

Angels and demons
Side by side in my brain box,
Like sticks of dynamite.

☾

Madhouse puppets,
Ventriloquist dummies
Dangling over the abyss.

What makes our arms
Go up and down,
Our trembling hands
Come together in prayer?

Cramped and dark as it is,
Old visionaries
May have left
Their broken toys
Here and there on the floor.

The red fire engine
Of my tongue
With a few wails
Still left in it.

This may be the dark dive
At road's end
Where my own heart comes served
In devil's dressing.

☾

I'm catching on, boss.
Mum's the word.
The voluptuous thrill of being nothing,
Must be *something*, eh?

Drawing a Blank

A bamboo cage on the sidewalk,
Two clairvoyant canaries,
Panchito and Estrella,
I was advised to choose between
Very carefully, so I picked her
To draw a card with my fortune—

A card that came up blank
On both sides, to the cheers
Of the onlookers, and the dismay
Of the street astrologer
Who hurried to offer me
Another draw, free of charge,

Making a big fuss, while I held on
To the blank one,
As the crowd swept me along
Into the whirl of streets and piazzas,
That Ferris Wheel of a day,
And late into the night

Winding down by myself in a café
Whose walls were antique mirrors
Where a decrepit, white-haired inebriate
Who introduced himself
As a doctor of philosophy,
Pondered its significance,

While I stole peeks at our reflections
Dimmed by the smoke of our cigars
Except for the card lying on the table,
Still unmarked under his dropped ashes.

The Inexplicable

How quickly it made itself at home
In our living room,
Which to all appearances looked no different,
Even when paid a surprise visit
By the inexplicable "something."

The fantastic animals in the carpet
And the mirror on the wall
That often sees around corners,
Waited for a nod that never came,
As we sat facing each other,

Reflecting separately what sort of courtesy
To extend to our guest,
While dust fell mote by fastidious mote
In the morning sunlight
As if being mindful of our silence.

We can feed it to the cats, I thought.
They'd know what to do with it,
And was at the point of saying so,
But did not, letting the inexplicable
Have its say, lover-like, in your ear.

Blind Typist

She stays late
To please her boss,
Working in the dark
Before a dark screen.

Her bony fingers
Like two white canes
With metal tips
Tap their slow way

It's something about you and me,
Something official,
A registered letter
We'll be wary to open.

For the love of God,
Be quiet
She's proofreading,
Her lips are moving.

She wears a rose in her hair
As she sits there.
The rose is red, of course.
Tock, tock, tock.

Death's Little Helpers

Even on Sundays we waited for them.
They'd knock on the door
Without bothering to look at the name.
In a book of photographs, I saw one of them
Stop to fire a pistol into the head
Of a child lying next to a rain puddle.
Its eyes were open and so were mine

The day I caught the eye of a cow
Between the slats of a cattle car.
I was crossing the tracks
In a great hurry to get somewhere.
The train had stopped mysteriously.
The engineer stuck his head out and waved.

I could hear the pistol shots.
Your hearing is amazing, people told me.
He's delusional, others said.
The dog paced around the room
Because he could hear it too.
After a while we all get used to things.
I never got used to it, so here I am awake.

We All Have Our Hunches

The child turning from his mother's breast
With a frightened look
To watch his grandfather raise a beer
And drink to his future happiness
In the kitchen full of unwashed plates
And busy women with quarrelsome voices,
The oldest of whom wields a rolled newspaper
With the smiling President's picture
Already speckled by the blood
Of warm-weather flies and mosquitoes.

Night Picnic

There was the sky, starless and vast—
Home of every one of our dark thoughts—
Its door open to more darkness.
And you, like a late door-to-door salesman,
With only your own beating heart
In the palm of your outstretched hand.

All things are imbued with God's being—
(She said in hushed tones
As if his ghost might overhear us)
The dark woods around us,
Our faces which we cannot see,
Even this bread we are eating.

You were mulling over the particulars
Of your cosmic insignificance
Between slow sips of red wine.
In the ensuing quiet, you could hear
Her small, sharp teeth chewing the crust—
And then finally, she moistened her lips.

Whispered in the Ear

Invisible friend, you have the air of a widower
Whenever I run into you on the street.
The two of us in matching raincoats,
Stiff-legged, wary of each other,

What do you do with yourself nowadays?
Consult the dictionary in the dark?
Kiss the Virgin in the empty church goodnight?
Tie beer cans to a parked hearse?

Once we shared a small pillow against the dark.
The infinite was all business
As it tucked us to sleep
In its blanket of zeroes.

Nothing to say to me now, chum?
A dull, sultry night upon us
Of canned laughter on TV
Spilling out of open windows onto the sidewalk,

Everybody lives the life they did not choose,
The empty streets said, and to further emphasize,
There was a sheet of greasy butcher's paper
The wind blew at my feet.

In the Courtroom

Not even a custodian's flashlight
So as not to trip on the way in.
And the lawyers' voices—
Like a midnight rustle of cockroaches.

If the judges are shrouded,
So is the accused.
Ghastly errors,
Mistaken identities are the rule.

A black, fingerless glove
Holding out a pale writ.
Something about a bug
Who lives a single day.

My heart risked a louder tick,
While His Honor mopped his forehead
With a handkerchief
I could not even see.

Do you hear that, Blind Justice?
I finally said in a loud whisper,
And then I bit my tongue
Which, to my surprise, tasted of blood.

Car Graveyard

This is where all our joyrides ended:
Our fathers at the wheel, our mothers
With picnic baskets on their knees
As we sat in the back with our mouths open.

We were driving straight into the sunrise.
The country was flat. A city rose before us,
Its windows burning with the setting sun.
All that vanished as we quit the highway
And rolled down a dusky meadow
Strewn with beer cans and candy wrappers,
Till we came to a stop beside an old Ford.

First the radio preacher lost his voice
Then our four tires went flat.
The springs popped out of the upholstery
Like a nest of rattlesnakes,
As we tried to remain calm.
Later that night we heard giggles
Out of a junked hearse—then, not a peep
Till the day of the Resurrection.

Wooden Church

It's just a boarded-up shack with a steeple
Under the blazing summer sky
On a back road seldom traveled
Where the shadows of tall trees
Graze peacefully like a row of gallows,
And crows with no carrion in sight
Caw to each other of better days.

The congregation may still be at prayer.
Farm folk from flyspecked photos
Standing in rows with their heads bowed
As if listening to your approaching steps.
So slow they are, you must be asking yourself
How come we are here one minute
And in the very next gone forever?

Try the locked door, then knock once.
The crows will stay out of sight.
High above you, there is the leaning spire
Still feeling the blow of the last storm.
And then the silence of the afternoon...
Even the unbeliever must feel its force.

Gas Station

At the end of a long dark stretch,
A bright orange sign in the night
Made us pull up to the pump
Where the two-lane road divides
The unknown into two halves,
Turn off the engine and wait
With our eyes on the empty office,
Its one naked, dangling lightbulb.

One of us ought to have gotten out
And hunted for the attendant,
Instead, we listened to the crickets,
And stared ahead at the trees
That had the air of waiting for something
Difficult to find words for
On a late summer night without stars,
With no town or house in sight.

The Unseen Hand

in memory of BILL MATTHEWS

It goes about its business,
Catching flies,
Letting them go as it pleases.
We do nothing.
We only note who's missing.

The bread from the table gone
And the old Italian waiter
Who brought us a new bottle of wine,
And his small white dog
Who followed him everywhere.

The bright sunny day stolen,
And that long happy year
As if it were confetti
In a young girl's hair,
Someone likewise pilfered.

Five-finger discount
Is what they call it on the street,
This short breather
Before the final snatch.

Interrogating Mr. Worm

So, this is the fool's paradise then?
The metaphysical costume ball?
The thick dictionary of blank pages?
The lavender soap bubble floating off toward the
    infinite
From the roof of the confetti palace?

I only have faith in you, Mr. Worm.
You are bashful and yet seem determined
As you go about your grim business
Underneath this hammock gilded by the setting sun
As it sways between the dark cypresses.

There's a carcass of a small animal
In the grass lush with wildflowers,
And the sound of an outdoor wedding party:
Cries and titters as the bride spins and falls
With a blindfold over her eyes.

Then, in no time at all, not even that.
A few raindrops is all it took
To restore the peace. You yourself,
I imagine, have taken cover
Already, using this short pause

To go over your appointments,
Cross out a few more names
In your address book as long as the daylight
Holds out against the June night
Now clearing and brimming with stars.

Another Doomsday Sect

There are just two of them
At the subway entrance
Obviously spooked
As they hand out leaflets

Wearing summer T-shirts.
In the cold millennial wind
His ribs show, and the nipples
Of her small breasts.

Since I'm a great sinner,
I also note her fingernails
Are bitten raw and her lips
Are stiff and blue with cold.

And then it's a quick dash
Down the steep stairs
Into the already shrieking,
Already burning familiar hell.

No One in the Room

And here I was asking
About a child
I saw on the street
Carrying an Easter lily.

It was spring then.
She came my way
In a crowd of turned backs
And emphatically
Blank faces,
With the eyes of someone
Who sees
Through appearances—
And she didn't like
What she saw in me.

Was it alarm or pity?
I always wanted to know.
No hurry replying,
I said to no one.
It's hot, and it's been years
Since I knew how to fall asleep.

The Lives of the Alchemists

The great labor was always to efface oneself,
Reappear as something entirely different:
The pillow of a young woman in love,
A ball of lint pretending to be a spider.

Black boredoms of rainy country nights
Thumbing the writings of illustrious adepts
Offering advice on how to proceed with the
        transmutation
Of a figment of time into eternity.
The true master, one of them counseled,
Needs a hundred years to perfect his art.

In the meantime, the small arcana of the frying pan,
The smell of olive oil and garlic wafting
From room to empty room, the black cat
Rubbing herself against your bare leg
While you shuffle toward the distant light
And the tinkle of glasses in the kitchen.

With Paper Hats Still on Our Heads

The check is being added up in the back,
As we speak.
That's why we don't see any waiters
Prowling around here anymore.
The rustle of bills you're counting
Makes me think of grass
Being mowed with a scythe in a graveyard
I don't reckon it'll be enough.

Dip your finger in what's left of the red wine
And let me suck on it slowly.
I wish they'd at least clear the dirty plates.
No prices on the menu
Should've been an instant tip-off.
Chitterlings in angel gravy,
How in the world did we ever fall for that?
Love of my life, start your jive.

I've Had My Little Stroll

Now, let me have a book-lined tomb
In some old cemetery
Where widows leave cigarettes and sweets
On the graves of their husbands,
And lovers come to solve the mysteries
Of each other's buttons.

Sitting, leaning against the stone
With a dog by my side.
Reading Emerson by candlelight,
Its yellow flame fretting
Like a caged bird.
Soul, what a lovely word!
My mind is as clear as a raindrop

Immense, gloomy heavens
With their amateur theatricals,
Cloud gesturing to cloud,
And then at first dawn-light
A child's cross like a seagull
At the edge of a distant surf.
Spreading its white wings.

The Cackle

Wee-hour world, insoluble world,
You may as well be a goldfish
Swimming in a bowl of ink
For all we understand of you.

Your small-beer philosopher,
Tinhorn preacher,
Chronic bellyacher,
Is about to die laughing tonight
With one final cackle

At the sight of a young couple
Slinking into the doorway
Of a grand old funeral home
Right across the street,
For some hot you-know-what.

SOME OF THESE poems have previously appeared
in the following magazines, to whose editors grateful
acknowledgment is made: *London Review of Books,
Tin House, The Southern Review, The Southwest Review,
Field, New York Review of Books, Grand Street, Boston Review,
The Missouri Review, The New Yorker, Five Points, Metre,
Thumbtack, Stand, Raritan, The Literary Review* and
Ploughshares.